99+ Ways to Save Money Now.

Copyright © 2018 by Tracy Hughes

All rights reserved. This book or any portion thereof may not be reproduced or used in any manner whatsoever without the express written permission of the publisher except for the use of brief quotations in a book review.

Printed in the United Kingdom

First Printing, 2018

Introduction.

Hands up if you remember the 80s. The time of Boom and not yet Bust, when your worth was based on how much you spent. Always having to have the latest, the biggest, the most expensive of anything.

Compare that with today, when people are trying to outdo each other with how cheaply they can buy things. Instagram feeds full of yellow stickers. Pinterest boards full of frugal tips.

And that is not a bad thing. We have become more aware now of the actual cost of things that we buy.

Bills are going up whilst salaries are remaining static so we know that we have to find ways to cut our costs and not rely on credit so much.

So here are more than 99 tips to save money and cut expenses covering everything from shopping to utilities to days out.

I hope you find some of them useful.

1. Bills, Budgets and Benefits

1.1 Calculate your monthly budget

Calculate your monthly budget so you know how much, if anything, you have spare each month. Just Google 'budget planner' and you will find many, many to choose from.

1.2 Make sure you know where all your money is going each month

If your budget is telling you that you should have money left over at the end of the month but you don't, then you need to find out where that money is going. Keep a spending diary for a month and list EVERYTHING you spend – from the newspaper and coffee on the way to work to the £5 you put into the office collection. You may be surprised to see where your money is going.

1.3 Pay by Direct Debit

Paying your bills by Direct Debit ensures that they are paid on time. It is convenient and you don't need time to find a bank or Post Office to pay over the counter. Some companies offer a discount, or at least some sort of incentive, to pay by Direct Debit. It also helps you with your budget as generally the payment will be the same very month.

1.4 Go paperless

In these more environmentally aware times, a lot of companies will give discounts if you opt to receive your statements and bills online instead of receiving a paper bill through the post.

1.5 Overpay your Mortgage

If you have any spare cash available, overpay your mortgage. Even a little bit extra will reduce the amount of interest you pay and may even reduce the term of your mortgage. Be sure to check the small print on your mortgage in case there is an early repayment fee to be paid.

1.6 Make sure you're on the best deal possible for all of your utility bills

Prices can fluctuate so much from company to company and even the company you're with will usually have more than one tariff so it's best to check every six months or so if you're on the best deal for your family. It's really easy to check – just have your bills to hand and use one of the many price comparison websites online to check the best deals. And don't forget that if you are thinking of switching, check with a cashback website like Quidco or TopCashBack.

1.7 Check that your house is in the right band for Council Tax

Apparently up to 400,000 houses in the UK have been assigned to the wrong Council Tax band and it's really easy to check if your house is one of them. If it is, you could have your future Council Tax payments reduced and get a rebate for any past overpayments.

You can check online what Council Tax band you and the rest of your neighbours are classified as. If you find that you're in a higher bracket than any of your neighbours (as long as they have a similar size house to yours) then you have a good case for asking your local council to arrange for your band to be reassessed.

1.8   Consider a water meter if you're not already on one

Do you have more bedrooms in your house than people living in it? If you do, the chances are you could save money on your water bills by getting a water meter installed. If you have a house full of people, a water meter may still save you money, or at least make you aware of how much water you are using. Water meters are usually free to install and allow water companies to charge you for the water you use rather than a flat rate which is based on the Rateable Value of your property.

1.9   Pay off your most expensive debt first

Obviously different companies will charge you different rates of interest on your debt, as you want to get rid of the debt as quickly as possible you should pay the minimum repayment on all but the debt with the highest interest rate, at this you should throw the minimum payment AND all the spare money you can afford.

There is another option here, and that is known as the Snowball Method. With this you put all of your spare money to the debt with the lowest balance. This method will allow you to pay off your smallest debt first, and hopefully quickly, giving you a little boost that you are one debt down.

The Snowball Method may mean you end up paying more than if you worked from the most expensive debt down but seeing the number of debts reducing may be the boost you need.

1.10 Take action if you cannot afford to pay

If you cannot afford to pay your bills don't just ignore that fact like a lot of people, including me, do or have done. The problem will not go away but you can act so that the problem does not become worse.

The first thing to do is to contact all of the companies you owe money to (your creditors) and let them know you are struggling. Some will be helpful, other companies less so, but you have nothing to lose.

The companies will need you to complete a table of incomings and outgoings so they can see what you can afford. If you have a budget already completed then you should have no problem completing any paperwork needed by your creditors.

1.11 Don't automatically renew Insurance Policies

Never renew Insurance policies without checking to see if there are cheaper deals available. These days loyalty does not always pay. I reduced my car insurance premium this year by swapping intermediary, last year my policy was with the Co-Op, this year I have saved a couple of hundred pounds by switching to the RAC. Both policies are identical and both are underwritten by the same company!

1.12 Save money with a single phone call

On the back of your credit cards there is a telephone number. Ring it and ask for a reduction in the APR you are being charged. You are the customer and they will want to keep you. You may be told no, but it hasn't cost you anything to ask.

Do this with your TV and Broadband providers and even your mobile provider. If you don't ask, you don't get.

1.13   Could you save with a balance transfer offer?

Do you have a credit card with a balance? Are you being charged interest on that balance? If so, and speaking to your card company hasn't helped, look for a balance transfer offer. Some card companies will offer you an interest free period on balance transfers. These can be from 6 months to 24 months. There will be a fee to transfer, generally about 5%, but if you have a large balance you can still save. You need to make sure that you have cleared the balance by the end of the offer period.

Again, you need to read the terms and conditions if you intend to spend on the card as well as using the balance transfer offer. Find out how the monthly payments are apportioned between the balance and any new purchases as you could end up paying more in interest overall.

1.14   Are you entitled to any Tax Credits?

A lot of people who have always been in paid employment do not realise that they could be entitled to additional help, particularly if they are in a low paid job. Take five minutes and complete a benefits check online today.

1.15   Where possible use cash.

Using cash makes you understand how much you are handing over, swiping a card to make a payment makes it feel less real.

2. Taxes.

Benjamin Franklin (1706-90), in a letter to Jean-Baptiste Leroy, 1789, wrote –

"'In this world nothing can be said to be certain, except death and taxes."

Successive Governments seem to love introducing new taxes, from a Window Tax back in the 18th Century, VAT so that the UK could join the Common Market in the 70s Governments just love to find new ways to take our money from us. Here are a few tips to fight back, a lot of these won't be relevant to many of us, yet, because if you are reading this you are probably in the same boat as me!

2.1 Check your tax code

Your tax code is a series of letters and numbers that determine what your personal allowance is. That's how much you can earn before Income Tax kicks in.

For most people in 2018-19, their tax code will be 1185L. This indicates that the taxpayer is under 65, earns less than 100,000 and so is entitled to £11,850 personal allowance before they begin paying Income Tax on their earnings.

You should double check your tax code each year to make sure you aren't on the wrong one, as you may then be paying too much to HM Revenue & Customs. If you find that more tax has been collected than you needed to pay, claim your money back! To do this you will need to contact HMRC in writing. You should enclose the relevant copies of forms like P60s and P45s, as well as an explanation of why you believe you are owed a refund.

2.2 Use your personal savings allowance

You can earn up to £1,000 in interest from savings without paying any tax.

The Personal Savings Allowance (PSA) is applied automatically and is £1,000 for basic rate taxpayers and £500 for higher rate taxpayers.

Current accounts, fixed-rate bonds and regular savers, NS&I investments, credit unions, peer-to-peer platforms, corporate bonds and Government bonds are covered by the PSA.

Given the low level of interest rates at the moment, you'd need at least £20,000 in a best buy savings account to even get close to exceeding the PSA for basic-rate taxpayers, but if you do manage to cross the £1,000 / £500 threshold, put your other savings in an ISA.

2.3 Open an ISA

The Personal Savings Allowance doesn't mean you should ditch your existing ISA or not bother opening one at all. That's because ISAs shield your savings from taxes over the long term.

The 2018/19 ISA allowance for adults is £20,000, which can be saved as cash and/or as stocks and shares. Children under the age of 18 also get a tax-free savings allowance with a Junior ISA. In 2018/19 children can put away up to £4,260 in cash and/or stocks and shares.

2.4 Invest in Premium Bonds

If you've used up your ISA allowance for the tax year but still have some money to put away, you could try National Savings & Investment Premium Bonds.

Premium Bonds allow you to save from £100 up to £50,000 and offer easy access to your cash. However, they aren't like normal savings accounts as they don't pay a regular return on your money. Instead, the interest that should be paid is used to fund a monthly prize draw, where bondholders can win between £25 and £1 million – or nothing at all.

Prizes are tax-free. And what's more, deposits are 100% backed by the Treasury.

2.5 Pay into a pension scheme

Auto-enrolment means that we (almost) all have a pension – but that doesn't mean you should be satisfied with making the lowest contributions. When you pay into a pension scheme you benefit from tax-relief on your contributions based on the highest rate of Income Tax you pay.

The way you get the tax relief depends on the type of scheme you belong to – in a workplace pension, your employer will deduct your contribution before you pay tax.

2.6 Don't blow pension savings

Pension freedom laws introduced in 2015 allow anyone aged 55 or over to take all of the cash from their pension savings, you can then do whatever you want with it.

However, withdrawing your whole pot could land you with a massive tax bill. Pension rules say you can take 25% of your pension pot as cash in one lump sum, or multiple withdrawals, tax-free. Any more than this will be taxed as income.

2.7 Stop paying National Insurance Contributions

If you continue working after reaching the State Pension age you no longer have to make National Insurance Class 1 and Class 2 contributions.

Make sure you stop these being taken from your wages by showing proof of age to your employer or writing to HMRC to get a letter confirming you have reached State Pension age.

2.8 Be proactive with Inheritance Tax planning

When you die, Inheritance Tax is charged at 40% on the value of your estate that exceeds £325,000 (£650,000 for people who are married, in a civil partnership or widowed, figures correct at the time of writing).

If you think your estate will be liable for the tax you should start making plans now to protect your wealth from the taxman and give more to the people you love.

One way is to make gifts of your money before you die (up to £3,000 per year). Leaving 10% of your estate to charity can also reduce your tax bill to 36%. There are other one-off gift allowances available too, but always take advice before going ahead with any such gifts.

2.9   Know your Capital Gains Tax rights

Capital Gains Tax (CGT) is payable on the profits made from selling assets like property, excluding your main residence, and any investments.

You don't have to pay if your gains are under your tax-free allowance. In 2018/19 the capital gains you can get tax-free is £11,700.

After the tax-free allowance CGT is charged according to your tax band. The rate of CGT for basic rate (20%) taxpayers has been cut from 18% to 10% and the rate for higher rate taxpayers (40% or 45%) has been cut from 28% to 20%.

However, the gains made on residential property sales aren't eligible for the new rates and the old 18% or 28% rates will still apply. Again, always take advice before doing anything.

2.10   Sharing economy tax relief

The Government has finally caught up with the proliferation of eBay, Gumtree and similar sites, with the launch of two tax relief schemes for the 'sharing economy'. The first £1,000 you make from selling your old stuff online, or items you've made, is now tax-free – beyond that, you'll have to pay income tax. (This is not including bought for resale items).

Additionally, the first £1,000 you make from your property, for things like renting out your driveway, is tax-free.

2.11   Use Stamp Duty exemptions

When you buy a house in the UK you have to pay a levy to the

Government called Stamp Duty Land Tax (SDLT). Stamp Duty is tiered and charged at different rates depending on the portion of the purchase price that falls into a band and higher rates now apply if your purchase is a second home or buy-to-let investment.

If you are buying your first home you now have access to extensive stamp duty tax relief. You'll pay 0% on the first £300,000 of the property value, then a reduced rate on the remainder up to £500,000. However, if the property price is above £500,000 you'll have to pay normal rate for the whole amount.

There is no Stamp Duty on residential properties bought for less than £125,000.

2.12   Take in a lodger

The Rent a Room scheme allows homeowners to take in a lodger and enjoy tax relief on rental income. This means that you do not pay tax on the first £7,500 you make in rent each year (or half if you share the income with someone else).

2.13   Get married

A bit drastic this one just to save a bit of tax!

Married couples and civil partners born after April 6, 1935, may be able to take advantage of a tax break called the Marriage Allowance. It allows a partner who earns less than £11,850 a year to transfer up to £1,190 of their personal allowance to their higher-earning spouse.

The Government estimates 4.2 million households could save up to £212 thanks to the scheme.

If you and your partner were born before April 6 1935, you may be entitled to Married Couple's Allowance instead of Marriage Allowance.

2.14   Trust your partner

You can transfer savings and investments to your husband, wife or civil partner to benefit from if they pay a lower rate of tax than you do.

However, it has to be a genuine gift. You can't ask for it back if you break up or change your mind.

2.15   Give to charity

The Government pays tax-relief on charity donations. Both you and the charity can benefit, but it depends on how you donate. Donating through Gift Aid means charities and community amateur sports clubs (CASCs) can claim 25p for every £1 you give back from the Government.

Higher rate taxpayers can claim the difference between the basic rate on the donation on their self-assessment return. Those that donate through a Payroll Giving (such as GAYE) scheme will donate from their gross wage or pension, so you'll then pay less tax on your remaining income.

And don't forget that those that donate more than 10% of their estate in their will get a reduced Inheritance Tax rate.

2.16   Stick to deadlines

If you have to file a self-assessment tax return, make sure you don't miss the deadlines as you'll be hit with an instant £100 fine and more charges will be levied the longer you leave it. If you are charged a fee you can always appeal.

The first year I had to file a self-assessment I didn't realise that it didn't go through correctly so when I received a fine three or so months later I contacted HMRC and explained and had the fine removed.

The deadline for paper returns is midnight on 31 October, but if you choose to file online you have until midnight on 31 January.

2.17   Offset expenses

Self-employed people and private landlords are allowed to deduct some business expenses before paying tax on their income.

Allowable expenses for the self-employed include travel costs, the running costs of business premises (including a home office) and buying stationery.

Meanwhile, private landlords can claim for things like agent fees, utility bills, maintenance, repairs, services like a gardener, legal fees and direct costs such as phone calls, stationery and advertising for new tenants.

They can also offset 50% of the tax on their mortgage interest and for wear and tear on their property, though the Government is reducing this particular tax break and will end it completely in 2020.

Landlords and those that run a business can also take advantage of the annual investment allowance (AIA) to claim tax back for capital expenditure on items such as tools and computers – the limit is currently £200,000.

2.18 Uniforms, work clothing and tools

You may be able to claim tax relief on the cost of repairing or replacing small tools you need to do your job (for example, scissors or an electric drill) and cleaning, repairing or replacing specialist clothing (for example, a uniform or safety boots).

You can claim either the actual amount you spend (keep your receipts) or an agreed fixed amount.

2.19 Fees and Subscriptions.

You can claim tax relief on fees or subscriptions you pay to approved professional organisations, (such as AAT, CIMA, ACCA etc), but only if you must have membership or it relates to your job.

You can't claim tax back on fees or subscriptions for life membership subscriptions or fees and subscriptions that you have not paid yourself.

3. Reduce Your Bills

Electricity and Gas

3.1 Unplug charges when they are not in use. If they are plugged and switched on they are using power even if the appliance is not attached.

3.2 Switch off appliances when not in use, leaving them on standby can cost up to £35 per year.

3.3 Use energy saving lightbulbs, although you don't really have much of a choice here. These bulbs use up to 80% less electricity than traditional bulbs and can last up to 10 times longer.

3.4 Don't fill the kettle just to make one cup of tea, just boil what you need. Alternatively, fill a flask with any remaining hot water if you are not sure how much you need, you can then use this for your next drink.

3.5 Fit a cylinder jacket to your hot water tank if you do not already have one, check any existing ones to see if they could benefit from being replaced.

3.6 Turn your thermostat down by 1 or 2 degrees, this can save up to £100 per year. Put a jumper on if you are cold.

3.7 If you have a loft, make sure it is insulated. Installing the insulation can cost around £300 but can then save you £100 per year. As insulation is expected to last 40 years, that's a pretty good return.

3.8 Wash at the lowest temperature you can, this is fine for all but the dirtiest of clothes. You can always do an occasional hotter wash, I work in hospital finance, if I have to go onto the wards for a meeting then that week my work clothes will be washed on a hotter cycle.

3.9 Ditch the dryer. As much as you can, dry your clothes naturally. Even in the winter line drying works, obviously windy weather works, but freezing temperatures work too. The cold temperature causes the moisture to form ice crystals which evaporate off when they are brought into the warm.

3.10 Keep the fridge and freezer full. Keeping these appliances full means they remain colder longer reducing the number of cooling cycles needed. Use bottles of water if you are nearing the payday big shop.

3.11 Keep the coils at the back of the fridge and freezer dust free. This allows the coolant to work more efficiently and remove the heat.

3.12 Invest in a slow cooker if you do not already have one. It uses less energy than a hob or oven, slow cooking for longer means you can use cheaper cuts of meat and being on all day means that it does actually help with heating the house during the winter.

3.13 If you are cooking on the hob use the correct size ring for the saucepan you are using. A small saucepan on a large ring wastes electricity by heating unused sections of the ring. A large saucepan on a small ring means the contents take too long to heat.

Water

These tips will save you money if you are on a water meter but will still help the environment if you aren't.

3.14 Take showers not baths. We all have times when only a bath will do but make these a treat not an everyday thing. This will reduce the amount of water you use AND reduce the cost of heating the water.

3.15 Turn off the tap when cleaning your teeth. This takes a bit of getting used to, it just feels weird. Or use the cold tap instead of the hot. Or do both.

3.16 Put a cistern displacer in your toilet tanks. These take up space reducing the amount of water the cistern holds, in turn reducing the amount of water used in each flush.

3.17 Use a watering can instead of the hose to water the garden. This will give you a bit of a workout as well as saving water.

4. Save when you're shopping.

4.1   Take it down a level.

If you currently buy a branded product, try the supermarkets 'finest' or 'best' range. If you are buying the 'finest' range, try the standard range and so on. If you can't tell the difference, or even if you can but are ok with it, then you are saving money.

This can apply to cleaning products and laundry detergent as well as food and drink.

4.2   Use Cashback sites.

If you are shopping online check to see if you can get cashback from sites like Quidco or TopCashBack. Some retailers have an agreement with these sites where you can register your debit card and you can get cashback by paying in store too.

Check out your bank account too, some now give cash back on purchases too every month.

4.3   Store loyalty cards.

Sign up to all the free store loyalty cards you can. Money spent in store adds points to your card. These are then translated into vouchers which means you can then get free stuff just for doing what you have to do anyway (such as buy food).

4.4   Check voucher sites.

Google vouchers sites these days and there are hundreds. You can also download Pouch to your laptop, Pouch recognises the site you are on and lets you know if there are any vouchers you can apply.

4.5   Check eBay.

These days retailers use eBay to sell new stock as well as used so you may be able to find a real bargain, new or used.

4.6   Start a gift cupboard.

If you see something in a sale that would make a great gift, buy it and put it away for later use. Cards too, that way you will always be ahead of the game.

5. Save on Food.

5.1 Meal Planning

I don't actually do this myself. As I live on my own and don't have to consider anyone else's tastes I tend to buy whatever food is reduced and base my meals around that. But, if you do have cater for more people, then meal planning is the way to go. You can save time and money by planning. You can go to the supermarket knowing exactly what you need to buy and you can get in from work at night knowing exactly what you are going to cook.

5.2 List what is in the freezer and pantry.

I have an A4 size magnetic whiteboard on the door of my freezer, on it I have listed by drawer what is in there. That way I can see at a glance what not to buy when I shop. I am working my way through my pantry doing the same too (I don't have a big pantry, it is just a bit messy at the moment).

5.3 Find out when your local supermarket reduces their stock.

The store on my way to and from work seems to reduce their stock twice a day, if I call in on the way to work there is always someone reducing dry goods, crisps and biscuits etc. When I call in on the way home, I arrive just as fresh vegetables, meat and bread are being reduced. Find out when your local store reduces their stock and try and do your shopping then.

5.4 Try online shopping.

Yes, there is a charge for this but it does remove the temptation of buying something that catches your eye, you have a list and you stick to it. However, it does mean that you cannot pick up any bargains, any of the instore reductions.

5.5 Use your leftovers.

Freeze your left overs and have them for lunch one day, take them to work and reheat them or eat at home if you are having a day by yourself. Prepare several meals from one piece of meat – for example a roasted chicken can make a traditional meat and two veg meal on the day of roasting, be eaten cold on a sandwich or salad the next day and the carcass can make soup or stock.

5.6 Grow your own veg.

These days vegetables can be grown in bags, hanging baskets and all sorts of containers so even the smallest balcony can provide some fresh veg. I currently have potatoes and tomatoes in bags and courgettes, carrots and chilis in raised beds. I also have two rhubarb plants which produce so much fruit that I end up giving it away.

5.7 Add lentils and pulses to bulk up meals.

Lentils and pulses are far cheaper than meat and can be used to add bulk to a meal if needed. Dried versions are cheaper than tinned but can take longer to prepare with some needing to be soaked for several hours.

6. Save around the house.

6.1 Old Fashioned Cleaning

Instead of buying different cleaning products for different jobs, take a leaf out of our Grandparents' book and learn how to clean using vinegar, bicarbonate of soda and lemon juice. A quick Google will tell you all you need to know.

6.2 Repair, don't Replace

If a button falls off, sew it back on. A hem comes undone, sew it up, or even use Wundaweb to iron hems back up. My Mum used to sew patches on the knees of my jeans and let them hems down on jeans and skirts as I grew to get more wear out of them.

6.3 Turn your bottles upside down

It can be surprising how much is left in an 'empty' bottle. When you think something is empty, turn it upside down and leave for a few hours, you should get another use out of it, maybe even more.

6.4 Don't Rinse and Repeat

Shampoo these days is much better at cleaning than the shampoos of years ago and will clean with one application. Brushing dry hair before you shower can also reduce the need for conditioners to prevent tangling.

6.5　Make and freeze baby food.

Don't waste your money on expensive organic baby food pouches, which can cost upwards of £1 each. It's so quick and easy to make your own, which can be frozen and used as necessary.

7. Save on motoring expenses.

7.1 Buy economical tyres

Need new tyres? While it might be tempting to go for the cheapest available, that can prove to be a mistake in the long run. Not only do such tyres not perform as well as more expensive tyres (tests show they often increase stopping distance and have a negative effect on handling), but they may also hit your fuel economy and need replacing more regularly.

Look out for is the tyre's EU tyre label. All tyres sold are fitted with one and it includes the fuel efficiency rating of the tyre. An 'A' rating means the tyre decreases the energy lost through the tyre (often referred to as 'low rolling resistance'), while a G rating is the worst performing - resulting in increased CO_2 emissions and fuel consumption.

Research conducted by Which? found that a good quality 'eco' or 'energy saver' tyre could improve fuel economy by around 2.5mpg compared with the worst tyre for rolling resistance. That could slash £50 off your yearly fuel bill, helping to offset the cost of buying good quality, premium brand tyres.

7.2 Don't pay extra for premium fuel

You've probably noticed the so-called 'premium' fuels when filling up with petrol or diesel. The retailers claim that these fuels offer performance and economy advantages, whilst cleaning and protecting your engine. In reality, unless you're driving a performance vehicle, you're unlikely to see any improvements by using fuel with a higher octane (petrol) or cetane (diesel) rating. You will, however, pay up to 10p a litre more for the privilege.

7.3 Don't press the accelerator when you start the car

Every car today has engine electronics that regulate the car starting procedure. In the olden days, you needed to use a little gas to get the car running - but you don't need to do this anymore. So, don't waste the extra fuel and risk damage to your engine by doing it, the car will start cleanly without.

7.4 Drive gently when the car is cold

Cars are at their least efficient when they are cold. If you drive quickly straight from start-up, you are redoubling the wasted fuel, and also wearing out the engine more quickly in the process. Show some mechanical sympathy and you'll immediately start saving money.

7.5 Don't let the engine idle too long

Today's engines are designed to operate from the moment you turn the key – warming the engine is no longer required.

If you like the car to feel warm on a cold day, it might be worth investing in a car with heated seats and a heated steering wheel. Remember to turn them off when you've warmed up, as they will increase your fuel consumption when switched on.

7.6 Check your tyre pressures

This simple check can save you big. OK, it might cost you 50p or £1 to do it at a filling station, but the savings soon add up. You could also buy an electric pump and check and inflate yourself, rather than go to a garage.

Tyres under inflated by 15psi - a difference you may not notice from a visual glance - can use 6% more fuel.

7.7 Take an advanced driving course

You can tweak your driving style to motor more economically. An advanced course will teach you these - you'll still make good progress but be doing it in a more efficient way. Hypermiling is the art of driving as economically as possible and once you take on the challenge, it can become addictive.

Advanced driving courses could also bring down the premiums on your annual car insurance policy.

7.8 Add family members to your car insurance

This is not 'fronting' as that is illegal. But adding your partner as a named driver on the family car can balance the risk and reduce your premium by a few pounds.

A word of caution: adding a young or inexperienced driver could increase your premium, as the insurer will base the cost on the driver with the most risk.

7.9 Use apps to find cheap parking spaces

Don't simply park up in the closest car park you can find, or the one you know the best. Check there isn't a cheaper one nearby first, using apps such as Parkopedia. Particularly in big cities, this can save you a fortune.

7.10   Park away from other cars

If your car is on finance, it will be assessed for condition before you hand it back. You'll be charged if any rectification is needed.

An easy way to reduce the risk of damage it to park away from other cars, so their car doors can't damage it, and they can't scrape it when driving in and out. Remember, even small car park panel dings are logged by the dealer on the condition report.

7.11   Don't use your windscreen wipers on ice

Windscreen wipers can cost £20 or more to replace. And they'll wear out much more quickly if you use them on ice in winter - you even risk tearing them entirely. Scrape the screen or use de-icer instead - this is also much safer (and less irritating for sleeping neighbours).

7.12   Empty your boot and ditch the roof rack

Don't carry unnecessary weight around with you. On average, every 50kg will increase your fuel consumption by 2%. A boot full of junk means you're using extra fuel for nothing. Emptying it out will give small savings that will add up the more you drive - particularly if your motoring is mainly stop-start driving and city commutes.

Remove your roof bars when they're not in use. Not only do they weigh between 3kg to 5kg, they'll also increase the amount of drag, increasing fuel consumption by about 10%.

7.13   Car share or use a car club

Do you really need to drive? Could you car share instead? You don't even need to know someone going in the same direction, services such as blablacar.com bring trusted carpooling to everyone. Simply enter where you are and where you want to go, and the service will hunt out available rides. You can even add your own car to the service.

Car clubs usually let you reserve cars via an online app, and you can often borrow them for anything from half an hour to a couple of days. Many clubs cost as little as 30p a minute or £5 an hour, or you can pay more for a bigger or more upmarket car. This includes all running costs including tax, insurance and even fuel.

7.14   Monitor your fuel economy

Do you know how many miles per gallon (MPG) your car returns under everyday driving? Don't rely on its trip computer - they're not always accurate - but use an app on your phone to calculate your MPG every time you fill up.

Once you know how well it performs, work out how you can improve it - and challenge yourself by making a game of it. Fuel efficient driving can save hundreds or even thousands of pounds at the pump over a year.

7.15   Wash your car yourself

Hand car wash centres are opening up everywhere. They charge just a few pounds and save you effort, so where's the harm? Well, even a £5 fortnightly car wash adds up to £120 a year but, doing it yourself will not only save you money, it will also allow you to keep an eye on the condition of your car and get any damage rectified before it gets too bad.

7.16   Get a black box insurance policy

A black box policy works by monitoring your driving via a small black box that's installed in your car. It builds a picture of the way you drive, allowing the insurer to treat you as an individual and reward safe driving with a lower premium.

If you are a young driver, black box insurance can be particularly helpful but you can also find more tips on our guide to making insurance cheaper for younger drivers.

7.17   Buy tax annually not monthly

You can pay vehicle excise duty (VED - or road tax) annually, monthly or every six months. Many go for monthly to split it into smaller payments, but it works out more expensive over the entire year.

For example, a petrol or diesel car with a tax band of D will cost £115 for 12 months if paid for in full, or £120.75 if paid by 12 instalments. Similarly, you'll pay £60.38 for six months or £63.25 if paid monthly.

7.18   Get a quote for comprehensive insurance - it may be cheaper

If you're on a budget, many assume third party insurance (the minimum legal requirement which only covers damage to other vehicles) will be the cheapest. But try getting quotes for fully comprehensive cover (which also covers damage you're responsible for to your own vehicle). The weird algorithm of insurance companies' computers often mean it's cheaper than third party.

7.19   MOT Tests

Look into whether your local council does MOT tests. They won't be able to carry out necessary repairs and therefore don't have a vested interest in finding faults.

7.20   Supermarket Fuel Offers

Keep an eye out for supermarket fuel offers – many will offer you money off per litre when you spend a certain amount on groceries.

8. Save on Days Out.

8.1 Book before you go.

It is generally cheaper to book online rather than paying on the gate, for instance Drayton Manor tickets are £39 per adult on the gate but buy up to the day before and you can get 4 adult tickets for £80, almost a 50% saving.

8.2 Check for workplace offers.

Does your workplace or union have any ongoing deals with local attractions. Working for the NHS we do get regular offers for free entry to places on particular days, ask your HR department, union rep or social club if you have one for any offers.

8.3 Check if the venue allows re-entry.

Contact customer services for wherever you are going, if they do allow re-entry then you can easily take your own lunch. Leave it in the car instead of lugging it around with you, pop out to eat and then get back to the fun. Obviously if you have a pushchair with you carrying stuff around is not an issue!

8.4 Consider purchasing a membership.

If you are regular visitor to an attraction, consider a membership. This can work out a lot cheaper. The advance price for 2 adults and 2 children for Chester Zoo is £95. A membership would cost £227 for the year, 3 visits and you have already saved money.

Membership also sometimes comes with perks, such as member only events or free gifts.

8.5   Check for off-peak reductions.

Check if you can purchase an afternoon only ticket, you will have less time to explore but if the discount is big enough, you may be able to go 2 or 3 times for the price of a standard ticket.

8.6   Team up and save.

How many people do you need for a bulk discount on tickets? Ask friends and family if they want to chip and buy a group ticket to save money. You can always split up once inside the venue.

8.7   Join the Sun Savers club.

Not only do you get £5 cash for every 28 codes you add from the paper, you can also take advantage of discounted holidays and free tickets to attractions. I have booked more holidays than I care to think about through the club and also had free tickets for Warwick Castle.

8.8   Visit a local park.

Go to your local park for the afternoon with a picnic instead of driving somewhere. Most will have a play park for kids and seating for adults to keep everyone happy. Plus, we all know how much fun can be had with an open space and a big stick.

8.9 Take your own equipment.

If you have it, take your own equipment to places such as the ice rink or squash court. Most centres charge extra for equipment hire so if you have your own and go regularly you can save yourself money in the long run.

8.10 Try Geocaching.

Geocaching is a great activity that will get you out into the big outdoors. It's an ideal way of getting the kids away from the Playstation or xBox and as it involves walking and finding caches it is a healthy activity that is very cost effective. If you have a GPS enabled device such as a handheld GPSr, PDA or GPS enabled mobile phone its free to participate in this great activity.

8.11 Visit a Museum.

All publicly funded museums in the UK are now free to enter, with 100s dotted up and down the country covering all sorts of topics there should be one near you.

www.ingramcontent.com/pod-product-compliance
Lightning Source LLC
Chambersburg PA
CBHW030541220526
45463CB00007B/2931